How the
LIGHT BULB
CHANGED HISTORY

How the
LIGHT BULB
CHANGED HISTORY

by Diane Bailey

CONTENT CONSULTANT

Paul Israel

Director and General Editor, Thomas A. Edison Papers

Rutgers University

ESSENTIAL LIBRARY OF
INVENTIONS

Essential Library

An Imprint of Abdo Publishing | abdopublishing.com

abdopublishing.com

Published by Abdo Publishing, a division of ABDO, PO Box 398166, Minneapolis, Minnesota 55439. Copyright © 2016 by Abdo Consulting Group, Inc. International copyrights reserved in all countries. No part of this book may be reproduced in any form without written permission from the publisher. Essential Library™ is a trademark and logo of ABDO Publishing.

Printed in the United States of America, North Mankato, Minnesota
052015
092015

THIS BOOK CONTAINS
RECYCLED MATERIALS

Cover Photo: Carol M. Highsmith/Library of Congress
Interior Photos: Janka Dharmasena/iStock/Thinkstock, 2, 68–69; The Print Collector/Alamy, 6–7; Daniel Dempster Photography/Alamy, 10; Corbis, 13; DIZ Muenchen GmbH, Sueddeutsche Zeitung Photo/Alamy, 14; iStockphoto, 17, 27, 88–89, 91, 99 (all); Bettmann/Corbis, 18–19, 28, 42–43, 53, 83; Dave Pickoff/AP Images, 22; World History Archive/Alamy, 26; North Wind Picture Archives, 29, 35, 40, 46, 56–57; AP Images, 30–31; H.C. White Co./Library of Congress, 37; Library of Congress, 39, 48, 65, 78–79; Red Line Editorial, 51; Bain News Service/Library of Congress, 55; Ernest Harvier/Library of Congress, 61; Schenectady Museum; Hall of Electrical History Foundation/Corbis, 66, (top), 66 (bottom), 76; Roger Wood/Corbis, 67 (top); iStock/Thinkstock, 67 (bottom), 95; Kirn Vintage Stock/Corbis, 75; Joe Potato/iStockphoto, 87; Pushish Donhongsa/iStockphoto, 96; Tom Roberts/The News–Gazette/AP Images, 98

Editor: Rebecca Rowell
Series Designer: Craig Hinton

Library of Congress Control Number: 2015930968

Cataloging-in-Publication Data

Bailey, Diane.
 How the light bulb changed history / Diane Bailey.
  p. cm. -- (Essential library of inventions)
Includes bibliographical references and index.
ISBN 978-1-62403-784-9
1. Electric lighting--History--Juvenile literature.   2. Inventions--Juvenile literature.   I. Title.
621.32--dc23
                                        2015930968

CONTENTS

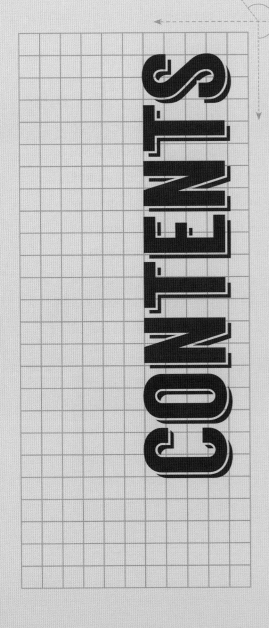

CHAPTER 1

FOURTEEN HOURS

Six weeks. In September 1878, Thomas Edison told the group of newspaper reporters who came to his Menlo Park, New Jersey, laboratory he needed six weeks. In that time, he would invent a reliable light bulb. Not only that, he would also create a power system that would make the light bulb usable.

Edison was already a famous and respected inventor when he made his declaration to the press. Among other things, he had invented the phonograph and improved the stock ticker. Even with his proven record as an inventor, Edison's goal for the light bulb was huge.

Thomas Edison in 1878. The phonograph was one of the many inventions he would create or perfect during his life.

THOMAS EDISON

Thomas Edison was born in Ohio in 1847. The Edison family moved to Michigan in 1854. Young Edison was a bright student and tended to exasperate his teachers with his constant questions. His mother took over the job of teaching him, and Edison later credited her with his interest in learning. Soon, he developed an interest in the sciences—as well as in making money. By age 12, Edison was selling newspapers and snacks on a nearby train that ran between Port Huron and Detroit. His interest in telegraphy and learning from telegraph operators along the railroad line led to his first telegraph job. Edison learned Morse code, a system of tapping in dot-and-dash patterns that correspond to letters. By age 16, Edison had come up with his first invention, a machine that would automatically transmit the Morse code used by telegraph machines. Edison never attended college, but he went on to invent many other machines, ultimately collecting more than 1,000 patents. His favorite invention was the phonograph, which could record and produce sounds. He married twice (his first wife died) and had six children. Two of them had the nicknames "Dot" and "Dash," after his work with Morse code.

The reporters returned to New York and published Edison's claim. When the news went public, the gas companies that supplied the fuel for the gaslights that lit most of the United States took a hit on the stock market, which tracks the financial worth of various companies. Then, everyone settled in to wait.

Six weeks passed. No light bulb.

Six months passed. No light bulb.

Finding a Filament

As the weeks and then months passed, Edison was far behind his original schedule, but he was not discouraged. He did not believe failure was a setback. Rather, he saw it as a necessary step on the path to success. This problem, however, had many thousands of steps.

Edison was not the first inventor to experiment with incandescent light. The idea was already 40 years in development by the time he turned his attention to it. Incandescent lights operate by passing an electric current through a material called a filament. The flow of electrons produces heat, and as the filament gets hotter, it glows. The whole apparatus is encased in a glass bulb from which the air has been removed. By creating this vacuum environment, the materials in the filament are unable to chemically react with the surrounding air and break down. The heat itself, though, causes the filament to deteriorate, and most of the early incandescent lamps lasted only a short time before the filament burned through.

These early light bulbs were novel, interesting things to look at, but they weren't very practical. No one could read a book or mend a shirt or do anything else useful in the few minutes some of the lamps provided light. The ones that did last longer were expensive to manufacture and distribute. Edison knew he had to find a way to make a working light bulb that would last considerably longer while also staying affordable. His first task was to create efficient vacuum

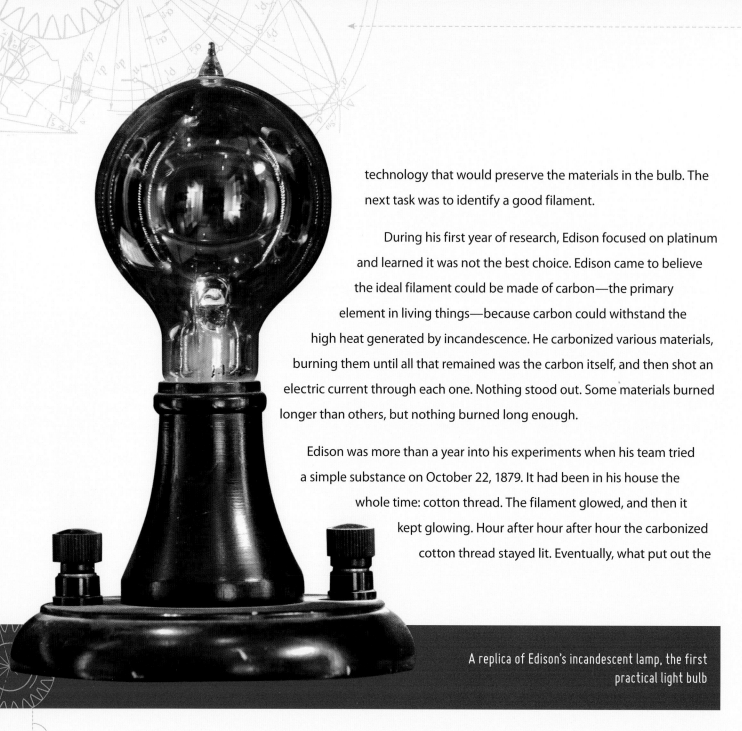

technology that would preserve the materials in the bulb. The next task was to identify a good filament.

During his first year of research, Edison focused on platinum and learned it was not the best choice. Edison came to believe the ideal filament could be made of carbon—the primary element in living things—because carbon could withstand the high heat generated by incandescence. He carbonized various materials, burning them until all that remained was the carbon itself, and then shot an electric current through each one. Nothing stood out. Some materials burned longer than others, but nothing burned long enough.

Edison was more than a year into his experiments when his team tried a simple substance on October 22, 1879. It had been in his house the whole time: cotton thread. The filament glowed, and then it kept glowing. Hour after hour after hour the carbonized cotton thread stayed lit. Eventually, what put out the

A replica of Edison's incandescent lamp, the first practical light bulb light bulb was not a fizzling filament but the bulb breaking. By then, it had been lit more than 14 hours.

Two months later, Edison was ready to unveil his new invention. Shortly after Christmas and into the new year, he gave demonstrations of his light bulb for reporters and the public. He may have underestimated how much time it would take, but he had succeeded in his goal to improve the light bulb.

The lamps Edison presented used cardboard filaments. They were cheap but not optimal in terms of life. The cotton thread had shown Edison carbon could work in his bulb. Next, he needed to find a more stable, long-lasting carbon material.

Simply Light

Over time, Edison steadily bettered his bulb. Cardboard was an improvement, lengthening the glow time to 100 hours. Eventually,

CHOOSING CARBON

With its resistance to high temperatures, carbon seemed ideal for making a light bulb filament. Plus, it was readily available because it is a fundamental ingredient in plant life. The team at Menlo Park believed filaments needed to be twisted and formed into spirals so a longer length of material could fit into a bulb. They thought the shape would be more energy efficient by keeping more heat in the spiral. But carbon was fragile, and it was difficult to form these carbonized materials into spirals. Edison's team experimented with straight lengths of carbon. These carbon wires demonstrated a naturally high resistance and were stable within the vacuum lamp. This simpler design proved successful in creating a working bulb.

BETTING ON BEARDS

As Edison searched for the perfect filament, he actually tried hair from the beards of two men working in his lab. The contest was enthusiastically followed. Employee Francis Jehl later wrote a book about his experiences working for Edison. He recalled, "Bets were placed with much gusto by the supporters of the two men, and many arguments held over the rival merits of their beards."[3] In the end, neither man had to shave his beard for the greater good—the hairs were not the solution.

Edison settled on carbonized bamboo, which was sturdier and extended the life of his bulb to 600 hours.[1]

The technology itself was amazing, but the revolutionary part was that Edison's bulb provided a kind of light people had never known. People were not accustomed to light arriving unaccompanied by sound, smell, and mess. The gaslights that served many people hissed as the gas ran through the lines, and the gas had a distinct odor. The soot it gave off meant lamps had to be cleaned often. Electric light did not come with the hissing sound of gas, the smell of kerosene lanterns, or the unreliability of flickering candles. Nor did it require striking matches, dipping wicks, or refilling fuel.

When Edison demonstrated his new light to reporters, they were struck by its low-maintenance nature and all the qualities it lacked. "There is no flicker," a *Washington Post* writer told his readers. "There is nothing between it and darkness. . . . It has no odor or color. [It is] simply light."[2]

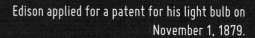

Edison applied for a patent for his light bulb on November 1, 1879.

To the Honorable Commissioner of Patents:

Your Petitioner Thomas A. Edison

of Menlo Park, in the State of New Jersey

prays that **LETTERS PATENT** may be granted to him

The Age of Electricity

The ability to see reliably and well, long after dark, changed the fundamental patterns of human life. Work hours got longer. Play hours got longer, too. Electric light illuminated places that had never been seen before, from the depths of oceans to outer space. It transformed industries that depend on quality lighting, including printing and photography.

People soon realized that electric incandescent lights were to be much more than simply light. The light bulb evolved during an era of unprecedented technological advancement and ushered in a new age powered by electricity. The first widespread application of electricity was lighting, which prompted the creation of an entire infrastructure that powered countless other machines—irons and vacuum cleaners, washers and dryers, radios and computers.

THE LONGEST-BURNING BULB

Since 1901, a light bulb at a fire station in Livermore, California, has been keeping the night at bay. In more than 100 years of operation, it has gone out only a handful of times due to power outages, earning it the *Guinness Book of World Records* title for the longest-burning bulb ever. The bulb has grown dimmer over the years, however. It began life at 60 watts but now runs at only 4 watts of power.

Even modern incandescent light bulbs are extremely inefficient. Approximately 10 percent of the energy is released as light, while the other 90 percent is given off as heat.[4]

Edison's work with the light bulb would change the world.

Not all changes were for the better. Constant light put new pressures on people to produce and be active. Sleep and general downtime were once mandated by the lack of light at night. Edison's advances with the light bulb downgraded the status of these activities, making them secondary to the well-lit march of progress.

Yet, overall, people embraced the benefits of Edison's bulb. Few things were so useful and so relatively cheap and convenient. Edison's light bulb began a chain reaction. Millions of people would follow his lead. They had literally seen the light, and they would never turn it off again.

An early sign reassured people entering a room lit with light bulbs: "The use of Electricity for lighting is in no way harmful to health, nor does it affect the soundness of sleep."[5]

THE LIGHT BULB

Early 1800s
English scientist Humphry Davy develops an electric arc lamp, which produces light by passing an electric current between two carbon rods.

1809
Davy creates an incandescent light.

1816
Baltimore, Maryland, becomes the first US city to install gaslights.

1841
Frederick de Moleyns discovers using a vacuum makes the light in a bulb last longer.

1857
Heinrich Geissler creates the Geissler tube, a gas discharge lamp that creates light by passing electricity through a gas within the tube.

1879
Thomas Edison invents the first practical incandescent light bulb.

1882
The first public power stations open in London, England, and New York, New York.

1886
The war of the currents begins when George Westinghouse begins using alternating current (AC) to compete with Edison's direct current.

1888
Westinghouse strikes a deal with Nikola Tesla to use the motor he developed that runs on AC.

1904
Inventors develop the tungsten filament to replace carbon filaments.

1935
President Franklin D. Roosevelt establishes the Rural Electrification Administration to bring electricity to homes.

1962
Nick Holonyak Jr. produces the first visible light from light-emitting diodes (LEDs).

1976
Edward Hammer creates the first compact fluorescent light (CFL).

2000s
The US Department of Energy aggressively pursues LED research to replace incandescent lighting.

2007
The United States passes legislation that requires more efficient light bulbs and eventually phases out traditional incandescent bulbs.

CHAPTER 2

OUT OF THE DARK

Humans learned to make fire hundreds of thousands of years ago. This was the first breakthrough in the quest for light, and until the 1800s, fire remained virtually the only way to produce light.

A candle, or a lamp lit with kerosene or oils from animals or vegetables, produced a small flame. Fire did not come instantly or easily. It required effort and constant maintenance. It gave light, but not without danger. It could burn someone's fingers—or take out an entire block of buildings. Using fire to light the night was both a

A kerosene lamp is one of the few
possessions of a poverty-stricken family
photographed in New York City in 1888.

SHADES OF DARK

For interior decorators in the Victorian times of the 1800s, every color started with the word *dark*. The color palette had dark red, dark green, dark blue, and dark brown, for example, all of which might be chosen because they blended so nicely with black. And avoiding black was impossible: the oil and gas lamps that lit the homes of the 1800s released a dirty black soot that settled into the fibers of curtains, carpets, and upholstery. The introduction of electric lights prompted decorating with lighter colors.

hazard and a luxury. People did use fire for light, but when the sun went down, it was easier, safer, and cheaper to go to bed.

The Industrial Revolution

The 1800s brought huge changes to the United States and some countries in Europe, including Great Britain. The population in Western Europe had surged at the end of the 1700s, and the greater number of people led to increases in manufacturing and commercially produced goods. There were also advances in transportation, chiefly led by the development of the steam engine in the first half of the century. This burst of technological growth, called the Industrial Revolution, changed European and US societies forever. Handcrafted goods gave way to ones produced on machines, and companies built large factories to meet the growing demand for consumer goods. Workers became concentrated in cities, moving by the thousands into the factory environments. As the pressure to produce increased, the need for lighting became acute.

The Industrial Revolution also saw breakthroughs in chemistry and physics. These helped lead to a better understanding of electricity. An important contributor to the field was Michael Faraday, an English chemist and physicist who studied electricity in the first half of the 1800s. His discoveries proved crucial for later developments in producing electricity using generators. Eventually, the social and scientific advancements of the 1800s would come together, producing both the market for electric light and the technological knowledge to produce it. Yet, in the early 1800s, practical electric light was still nearly a century in the future. The cutting-edge technology of the time was gas.

Flammable gas, usually made from coal, was piped through central lines to lamps placed along streets. For decades, lamplighters made their rounds, lighting the lamps at sunset and extinguishing them at dawn. Eventually, the technology made its way inside houses. But gaslights were smelly, dirty, and often dangerous. Home lighting still had much room for improvement.

Electric Experiments

In the early 1800s, Humphry Davy, an English inventor, produced an electric light called an arc lamp. Rather than having a bulb and a filament, as incandescent lights do, Davy's arc light worked by passing an electric current between two carbon rods placed a few inches apart. The moving electrons created high temperatures that vaporized the carbon, and the carbon vapor emitted a bright arc of light as it passed between the rods.

Arc lamps were the first kind of electric light, but they had several drawbacks. They were much too bright for indoor use, and they were bothersome to operate. The carbon rods lasted only a few hours before they burned out and had to be replaced, and the rods had to be placed just the right distance apart—approximately four inches (10 cm)—for the arc to work. If the rods were too far apart, the current could not make the jump between them and the light went out. If the distance was too short, not very much light was produced.

By the late 1870s, shortly before Edison began his work on incandescent lights, arc lights were being used on city streets and in other outdoor applications, but they were far too powerful for indoor use, shining with the brightness of thousands of candles. And while gaslights were commonly inside houses, they were messy and dangerous. The search for the perfect indoor light was under way.

HUMPHRY DAVY

Born in 1778, the English chemist Humphry Davy was one of England's leading scientists in the early 1800s. His work led him to realize the production of electricity depended on chemical reactions taking place. As a result, he became a pioneer in the new field of electrochemistry, which studies the relationship between electricity and chemistry. One of his areas of study was electrolysis, the process of using an electric current to force a chemical reaction. Using a battery—a technology that had been invented in 1800—he was able to use electrolysis to isolate and identify certain elements, including sodium, potassium, calcium, and magnesium. One of Davy's students was Michael Faraday, who went on to become one of the most influential chemists of the 1800s.

In 1960, an old gas lamp still burned in New York City's Greenwich Village.

In the 1800s, many shipping disasters were not the result of storms or choppy seas. Rather, not being able to see in the dark caused many catastrophes. Oil and gas lamps were no match for dense fog or deep night. In the 1860s, the maritime industry was among the first to adopt powerful arc lights, which were visible for much greater distances. Installing arc lights on ships and in lighthouses helped ships avoid running into rocks, reefs, and each other.

The Incandescent Light

The incandescent light seemed the answer to this problem. As electricity flowed through a filament, it created a gentle glow—neither too dim nor too bright. Several inventors worked to advance this technology. In addition to his work with arc lights, Davy also built an incandescent light in 1809 using a filament made of platinum. In 1841, Englishman Frederick de Moleyns also used platinum wires, but he made an important improvement: he put them in a vacuum, inside a glass globe. The vacuum was an important step in the development of the incandescent bulb. If the bulb had ordinary air inside, the material in the filaments would chemically react with the air. The by-products would build up on the inside of the bulb and darken it. In addition, the filaments would burn out more quickly. Removing the air to create a vacuum would slow this process and make the light last longer. But it took years for vacuum technology to improve, and most early light bulbs did not use it.

Other inventors were also working on developing better light bulbs. The English inventor Joseph Swan made one using a carbon filament in 1860. But he created only a partial vacuum within his bulb, so it burned out too fast. Later, after vacuum technology improved, Swan tried again. He demonstrated his light bulb shortly before Edison did, but the thick carbon rods he used were not high resistance and burned through too quickly, making them uneconomical.

American engineers William Sawyer and Albon Man also developed a light bulb using a carbon filament—and they also did it before Edison. But they had used different kinds of carbon than Edison. Their technology did not work as well as Edison's bamboo-filament bulb. Disputes over who should hold the patent wound through the court system for years, and Edison eventually triumphed.

Edison's Bulb

A tireless experimenter, Edison reached a few important conclusions about what was needed to make an effective and economical light bulb. One had to do with creating a vacuum inside the light bulb. Like other inventors, Edison

FLAWS REVEALED

The soft yellowish glow of gaslights concealed imperfections in people's appearances. But the harsh glare of arc lamps, with their bright, bluish-white hue, highlighted every pimple, wrinkle, or gray hair. The light tended to make people look washed-out and sickly, especially those with lighter skin tones. After having their flaws exposed under arc lamps, some people wrote off electric lights entirely.

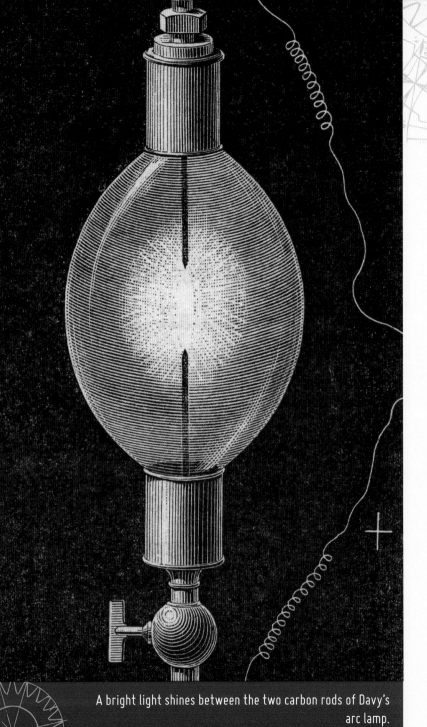

A bright light shines between the two carbon rods of Davy's arc lamp.

had experimented with platinum filaments. While conducting this research, he realized the platinum was absorbing hydrogen from the air, which lowered its melting point. Thus, one of Edison's lines of research was to create an almost total vacuum within his bulb.

Edison also knew he needed to use a filament with a high resistance. The reason had to do with both economics and the nature of electricity. Edison was thinking about more than his light bulb. He also contemplated a system that would distribute electricity to people. After all, his bulbs would be useless without the electricity to power them. Lines that would carry the electric current through the streets were made from copper, but copper was

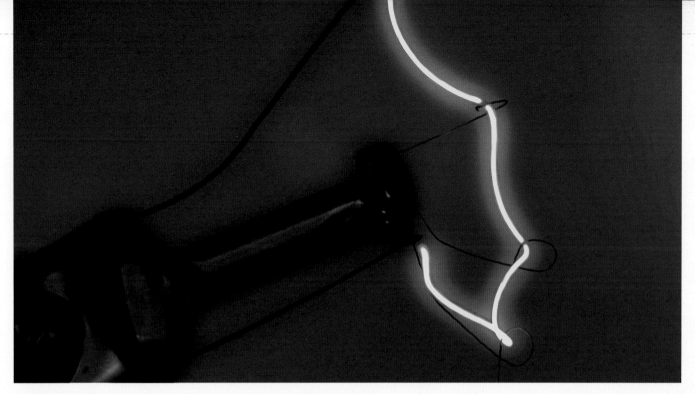

Edison's work with filaments led to a successful incandescent bulb.

expensive. Using thin copper lines would be far cheaper than using thick ones, but there was a catch: they could carry a low current only.

At this point, Edison turned to Ohm's law. Named for German physicist Georg Ohm, who published his findings in 1827, the law defined how the different components of electricity worked together. In electricity, the current is the rate of electron flow—the number of electrons that pass a certain point in a second. The voltage is the force that moves the electrons from one point to another. Resistance is the friction that slows down the electrons during their journey.

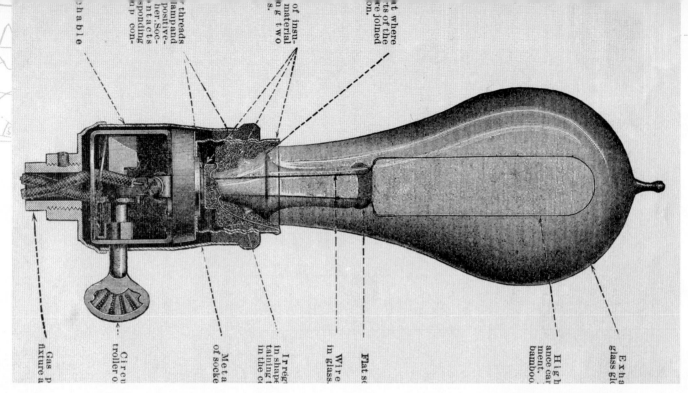

Labels around the diagram (partial, cut off at edges):

t where
ts of the
re joined
on.

of insu-
material
ng two
s.

threads
lamp and
positive-
her. Soc-
ntacts
sponding
p con-

chable

High
ance car-
ment,
bamboo.

Exha
glass glo

Gas p
fixture a

Circu
troller o

Meta
of socke

Irreg
in shape
taining i
in the c

Wire
in glass.

Flat s

Edison's incandescent lamp came together as a result of his determination, ingenuity, and the work of inventors he built on.

Ohm's law states that voltage is equal to the current multiplied by the resistance. When Edison did the math, he concluded that using a low current would require a material with a high resistance. That way, he could keep his copper costs down.

Edison's name is indelibly associated with the light bulb, but his experiments and innovations rested on the shoulders of many who came before him. Several inventors were in a close race to claim the rights to the "first" light bulb. In reality,

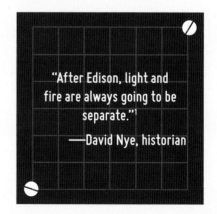

"After Edison, light and fire are always going to be separate."[1]

—David Nye, historian

no one person deserves all the credit. Many people had worked for years, building on the technology little by little. A combination of factors put Edison in the spotlight. Part of it was hard work. Part of it was good timing. And part of it was Edison's vision. He viewed the light bulb as just one rung on a long ladder, and he wasn't content to stop at building the bulb itself. In the quest to outshine his competition, he had much bigger plans.

The design for the light bulb's screw base also came from Edison. He got the idea while unscrewing the lid of a can of kerosene.

The work of German physicist Georg Ohm helped Edison achieve success with electric lighting.

CHAPTER 3

POWER TO THE PEOPLE

In theory, the incandescent light seemed to solve the perennial problem of lighting the dark, and it did so while also resolving the issue of smell and mess that came with using gaslights. It was less harsh and easier to maintain than its electric counterpart, the arc lamp. Edison had already connected wires and filaments until he bridged the gap between theory and reality. Now, he had an even more difficult connection to make—the one between reality and practicality.

A lone light bulb, even one that could work for several hours, was of little use in the 1800s because the technology could not

In 1880, workers pose at Edison's Menlo Park facility, the first factory to manufacture bulbs commercially.

operate on its own. In addition to needing skilled glassblowers to make each bulb, the bulbs then needed a socket and wiring. This required an electrician in an age when electricians did not yet exist. Most of all, a light bulb needed a power source to operate.

Isolated Lighting

The most visible and awesome part of Edison's creation was the light bulb itself. But the bigger part of the puzzle was less thrilling, but maybe even more difficult. Edison's goal was to establish central power plants that could supply electricity and lighting to numerous people simultaneously. His vision, in essence, was the forerunner of the grid, the vast infrastructure that now supplies lighting throughout the United States. Building such technology was a daunting task. Not only would Edison have to overcome technical hurdles, he also required money from investors who believed in what he was doing.

To build support for the project, Edison formed a company to install smaller, independent systems for private companies and wealthy individuals. These isolated systems operated with the same basic principles as the larger system he envisioned, but they were self-contained. A generator to produce the electricity was installed on the premises and then wired to the lights. Edison installed his first isolated system in 1880, on the steamship *Columbia*. Hundreds more followed, but these systems were still available only to people who had the money to pay for them. Edison wanted to create a centrally located system that could make electricity available to many people.

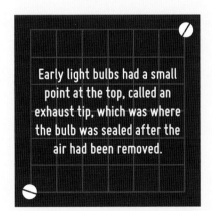

Early light bulbs had a small point at the top, called an exhaust tip, which was where the bulb was sealed after the air had been removed.

London Lights Up

The obvious choice for such a system was New York City, which was densely populated and conveniently located near Edison's New

Jersey headquarters. Edison received permission from city authorities to begin the project, but digging up the ground to lay electric wires was a slow and expensive process. Many people doubted it would ever work. Even as workers slogged away in New York, Edison agreed to another project. This one would be quicker and easier, and it would help demonstrate the viability of a central system.

Across the ocean, Edison's representatives visited the city of London, England, which was eager for electric lights. City authorities contracted with Edison's London company to install a central system under Holborn Viaduct. The viaduct was ideal: it was basically a bridge with buildings on top, and the wires could be installed underneath the bridge without having to dig underground. As a bonus, the location was near Fleet Street, London's central newspaper district, so reporters could easily view the installation and publicize it.

The station opened in January 1882, but that same year, Great Britain passed a law severely limiting how the infrastructure needed to support central power stations could develop. Edison was unable to expand his network. This act thwarted the spread of electricity in the country for years. In fact, most of Europe lagged behind in the switch to electric light. Cities there installed some electric lighting, but much less than in the United States.

Edison helped bring electricity to London.

Power Comes to Pearl Street

Edison had proved his point with the Holborn station in London, and his bigger goal, New York, was not far behind. His team had chosen a site on Pearl Street. From this location, generators—also called dynamos and jumbos—would produce electricity, which would then be transmitted up to a half mile (0.8 km) away. Within that half mile were the perfect customers. Pearl Street Station was situated near Wall Street, the heart of New York's financial district, and close to newspaper offices, just as with the Holborn station. The first beneficiaries of the new system would be rich and influential businessmen such as financier John Pierpont Morgan, who had invested in Edison's company, and newspapers such as the *New York Times*, which could sing the praises of Edison's project from its electrically illuminated offices.

By the autumn of 1882, a year and a half had passed since Edison had signed the contract for the New York project. Most of the time had been consumed by difficult digging and setbacks due to bad weather and interruptions in deliveries of supplies. Nearly $500,000 had been sunk into this new business.[2] Problems arose at every turn. "Everything is so new that each step is in the dark," Edison said. "I have to make the dynamos, the lamps, the conductors, and attend to a thousand details the world never hears of."[3] At one point, the underground cables had not been properly insulated and electricity "leaked" into the streets above, shocking horses on the pavement. Edison himself was nervous

Edison poses by a dynamo.

LIGHT BULB LINGO

With time, the vocabulary of the electric light became part of everyday speech, where it remains. A smart person is described as "bright," whereas one who is deficient in intelligence is a "dim bulb." When a difficult concept is grasped, or a realization made, "the light goes on." Even back in the 1890s, an energetic or easily excited person got termed a "live wire." Light bulb lingo may eventually vanish from the lexicon, but it likely won't happen at the flip of a switch.

about the project's eventual success, saying, "What might happen on turning a big current into the conductors under the streets of New York no one could say."[4]

The test of Edison's big idea came on September 4, 1882. One of Edison's engineers, Edward Johnson, tried to ease the tension with a joke. "One hundred dollars they don't go on," he said. "Taken," Edison snapped back.[5] Edison flipped the switch and became $100 richer.

Getting the Word Out

A single dynamo went online that first day on Pearl Street, lighting approximately 400 bulbs. By the end of the year, three more generators joined the lineup, powering approximately 5,000 bulbs. By 1884, the output had doubled again, to 10,000 bulbs.[6] Nonetheless, the spread of Edison's plants throughout the country took time.

Attracting investors to fund expensive central stations was difficult. To help promote his technology, in 1883, Edison established a company that focused on designing systems for smaller towns, showing the viability of his invention. He also employed a few public relations tricks. For one stunt, he had men march in a parade wearing helmets with light bulbs fitted to them. In the 1880s, such a sight was amazing. People still equated light with fire and the dangers that came with it. The marching men, however, demonstrated that electric light was perfectly safe—safe enough to wear.

Finally, electric light systems began catching on. By 1891, Edison's company had installed more than 1,300 central power plants across the United States, with a combined total of approximately 3 million lights.[7]

But Edison's company was not alone in the endeavor. By 1885, the desire for electric lighting had spawned more than 600 competing companies,

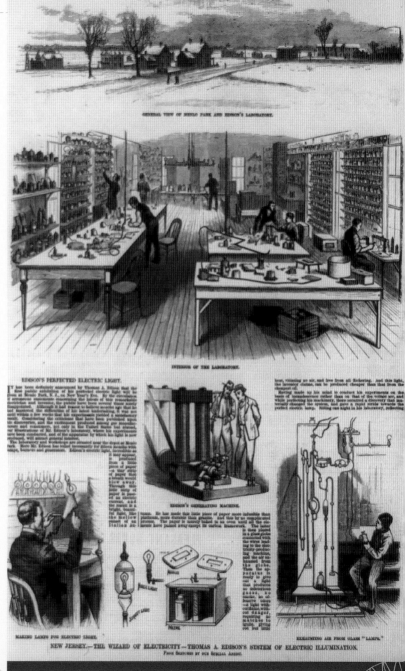

Six views from Edison's world, including Menlo Park, workers, and a light fixture.

for both arc and incandescent lights.[8] The rivalry was fierce, and unsuspecting customers had trouble sorting through the thick rhetoric used to rope them in. One contemporary observer wryly joked, "There are two kinds of electric lights, namely, our kind and the other fellow's kind. Our light is much better than the other fellow's light. The other fellow's light is surrounded by a cloud of non-luminous verbosity."[9] In other words, there was a lot of talk that did not mean much.

In fact, most of the industry struggled with itself. Battles ensued over safety concerns, inventors got into tugs-of-war over patents, and companies struggled to establish a niche in the market. Electricity would eventually change from novelty to necessity, but there were many obstacles to overcome in the process. Some were about safety, some were about technology, and some were about tradition.

SETTING STANDARDS

In 1884, several manufacturers pitted their bulbs against one another to see which was best. The event was sponsored by the Franklin Institute, an organization devoted to encouraging the development of scientific knowledge. A watchman stood guard as light bulbs from four competing companies were lit up in an endurance contest. Tests developed by the institute measured how well each was doing. Edison's bulbs carried the day, still burning after 1,000 hours.[10]

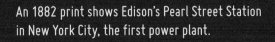
An 1882 print shows Edison's Pearl Street Station in New York City, the first power plant.

CHAPTER 4

THE FIGHT FOR LIGHT

In October 1859, an electricity worker named John Feeks climbed into a tangle of electric wires hanging above streets in New York City. He lost his balance, lunged for a line to catch himself, and was electrocuted by the high-voltage current being used to illuminate the street's arc lights. On the street below, people watched, horrified, as his body convulsed and caught fire. There was no way to get him down easily, and his dead body dangled in the wires for close to an hour before the power supply could be cut off and his body retrieved.

An illustration depicts electricity as dangerous—a deadly demon—a message gas companies spread in an effort to keep customers.

SAFETY FIRST

Digging up New York's streets to install the wiring for his new central station came with many challenges for Edison, one of which was safety. Electricity was so new that few people understood it, and even his workers were nervous about the dangers of the "devil in the wires."[1] To relieve fears, Edison designed a safety fuse, which he patented in 1890. The fuse would interrupt a current that got too strong and threatened to overload the circuit, possibly starting a fire. He demonstrated the fuse to the New York Board of Fire Insurance Underwriters to convince authorities his system was safe. Edison's successful demonstration prompted the organization to endorse it.

The Dark Side of Light

Feeks's story was not unique—other people had also died in electricity accidents. Nonetheless, dozens of people had witnessed the grisly scene, which fueled the debate about safety. The convenience of electric light had to be weighed against its risks. Electric wires could—and did—come tumbling down, and sometimes injured or killed people. Other risks came from wiring that was improperly insulated, which could result in its electric current leaking out and shocking people on the streets above. Another problem was that sparking wires could cause fires.

In November 1889, on Thanksgiving Day, the *Boston Herald* newspaper proudly proclaimed that the Massachusetts city's downtown—now electrically lit—was safe from fire. The next week, electric wires overheated and started a fire in a warehouse packed with dry goods. The fire spread throughout the day, jumping from building to building, and destroyed a large portion of the so-called fireproof downtown. The fire caused millions of dollars in property damage. A fire inspector blamed the disaster on the electric system and prompted the city to impose stricter oversight. Clearly, electricity was not entirely safe. The bigger issue was whether it was safer than its competitor, gas.

Battling the Gas Companies

In the late 1800s, the United States had been lit with gas lighting for several decades, and the gas companies enjoyed a comfortable monopoly. The industry was worth hundreds of millions of dollars, and its bosses had no intention of letting electricity take over as the dominant power supply for lighting. A fight between gas and electric companies ensued as representatives from both industries attacked each other and claimed to have the best, safest technology.

STAYING HOT

The gas industry had one major advantage over electricity: seniority. The industry was well-established, with a far-reaching infrastructure and the financial resources to explore other options. Diversification proved key to the survival of the gas industry. Gas could be used for more than lighting; it was also ideal for heating and cooking, applications that were unsuited to the infant technology of electricity. Electricity eventually made inroads into these fields, but a large proportion of US homes still depend on gas for these uses in the 2010s.

The gas companies knew arc lighting was a challenge to their business, but they also knew their situation was not as bad as it could have been. Stunningly bright arc lights only suited outdoor areas. They were for football stadiums, not dining rooms. Millions of private homes and businesses were still the purview of the gas companies.

The incandescent light was a different threat altogether. The amount of light was neither too bright nor too dim but just right. Plus, light bulbs were easy, clean, and convenient.

Nonetheless, electric lighting companies knew battling the gas companies would be tough. The gas industry was firmly entrenched, and users were familiar with the product. The gas companies had plenty of money to wage war against the electricity industry. Perhaps, though, they had too much money.

When any one company or industry has a monopoly, some customers end up feeling disgruntled, unhappy with the lack of choice and the ability of the industry to control access and prices. Many people had long been convinced they were being cheated by the gas companies, but with no competitor to turn to, customers were left with little recourse.

That changed in the mid-1880s. Spearheaded by Edison, the electric light went after the gas companies on several fronts. Edison said of the gas companies, "[They] were our bitter enemies in those days, keenly watching every move and ready to pounce upon us at the slightest failure."[2]

When it came to the quality and convenience of the light, electricity won hands down. That left two major battlegrounds: cost and safety. Edison crunched the numbers tirelessly, looking for ways to cut his costs so he could sell his product at a price that was competitive with gas. Light bulbs were expensive. It cost him approximately $1.40 to

By 1888, electricity lit up New York City, where residents could see election results broadcast in bright lights.

LIGHT THROWN ON A DARK SUBJECT.

(Which is Bad for the Gas Companies.)

make one bulb (approximately $33 in 2014), but they sold for 40¢ (approximately $10 in 2014).[3] Edison sold the bulbs at a loss for one simple reason: not enough people would buy them at the high prices. If Edison wanted to establish his new industry, he had to give customers some financial incentive.

Edison also began a campaign of public relations to emphasize the dangers of gas. Gas killed. The proof was in the stories and statistics, which reported on innocent and trusting users who were asphyxiated, or suffocated, by leaks of the poisonous fumes or died ghastly deaths in fires and explosions. The gas companies retaliated by slashing prices, coming up with better technology, and publicizing their own horror stories of electrocutions, but in the end, they could not triumph over the electric light.

DC and AC

An even bigger battle awaited, hinging on the science of how electricity worked. It would pit Edison against Nikola Tesla, a Serbian engineer, and George Westinghouse, a Pittsburgh businessman. The key was a simple multiplication problem: the total amount of power provided by electricity is equal to the voltage, or the pressure moving the electrons, multiplied by the current, or flow of electrons. Current is measured in units called amperes (amps). Lower voltages needed higher current, or more amps, and higher voltages needed less current, or lower amps, to get the same amount of power at the end.

An 1878 drawing has Edison shining his new bulb on two men with gas-meter heads, symbols of the then-powerful gas companies.

Edison's electric system used direct current (DC). Because it was delivered at relatively low voltages, DC was safer than gas. DC, however, was not efficient. The higher current produced more heat, so more of the available energy was lost as heat.

Pearl Street Station pumped out DC electricity at 110 volts. That number instantly began to decrease as the electricity traveled, but because the station only served businesses located within a half mile (0.8 km), the drop was not enough to make a meaningful difference. In other words, because the electricity did not have far to travel, it had little opportunity to lose power along the journey. While this was good news for Pearl Street and cities in general, it could be a problem in small towns or remote areas that were not situated next to a power station.

While Edison was devoted to his DC systems, others wanted to find a way to transport electricity over long distances without it losing its juice. The answer to this dilemma lay in using a different method of delivering electricity, alternating current (AC). Alternating current had an important advantage: unlike direct current, which worked on a fixed voltage, it was easier to manipulate its voltage. Power companies could raise the voltage of AC and simultaneously lower the current. A higher voltage was more dangerous, but the lower current that came with it also meant thinner, cheaper distribution lines. Using AC, power companies could send large amounts of electricity at high voltages over long distances without breaking the bank by building thick power lines. Then, when the electricity

DC SYSTEM VERSUS AC SYSTEM

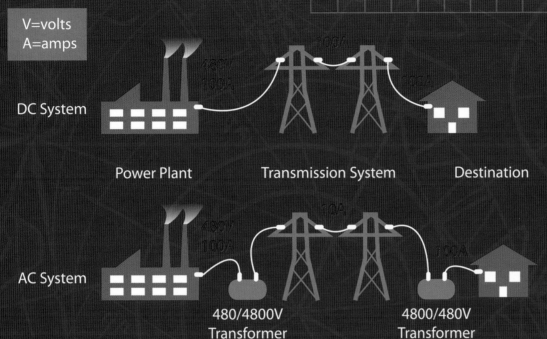

V=volts
A=amps

DC System

AC and DC require different systems to work. Both require a power plant and power lines to get energy to consumers. AC systems also require transformers that decrease the amps, or current, for transmission through the power lines and then increase it for use at the final destination.

Power Plant

Transmission System

Destination

AC System

480/4800V
Transformer

4800/480V
Transformer

reached its destination, it passed through a transformer that brought the voltage back down to a safe level for use by customers. Today, most electricity is delivered to customers using AC. It might travel long distances at an extremely high voltage, say 120,000 volts, and then be reduced to 120 volts when it is delivered into homes.

NIAGARA FALLS

A primary battlefield of the war of the currents was at Niagara Falls, the powerful waterfalls that straddle the border between the United States and Canada. The massive power of the falls could be captured in hydroelectricity, using the force of the falling water to power generators that produced electricity. Authorities in charge of Niagara sponsored a contest designed to see who could make this happen. General Electric was one competitor, with a proposal that used a combination of AC and DC delivery. George Westinghouse and Nikola Tesla also competed, proposing an AC system that was ideal for Tesla's AC motors. This plan won out and became the standard in the United States. In November 1896, Niagara's power reached the town of Buffalo, New York, 26 miles (42 km) away.

The War of the Currents

Edison vehemently opposed AC. He cited safety issues, arguing that the higher voltages used to transport AC electricity were more likely to cause a fatal electrocution. He claimed that AC killed and should be banned in favor of DC. But it is likely that part of Edison's concern was self-serving: AC was in direct opposition to the infrastructure he had spent years developing.

Westinghouse agreed with Edison on one point. "Yes, the alternating current will kill people," he conceded. But, he added, "So will gunpowder and dynamite and whiskey."[4] His point was that AC was safe if used properly. And Westinghouse was eager to compete with Edison and share in the lucrative electricity market. He began installing AC systems across the nation in 1886, bringing power to remote areas.

A problem remained, however. Electricity was being used for things other than lighting, and most electric motors depended on DC.

In 1888, belts drive the machinery in an early AC power plant by Westinghouse Electric.

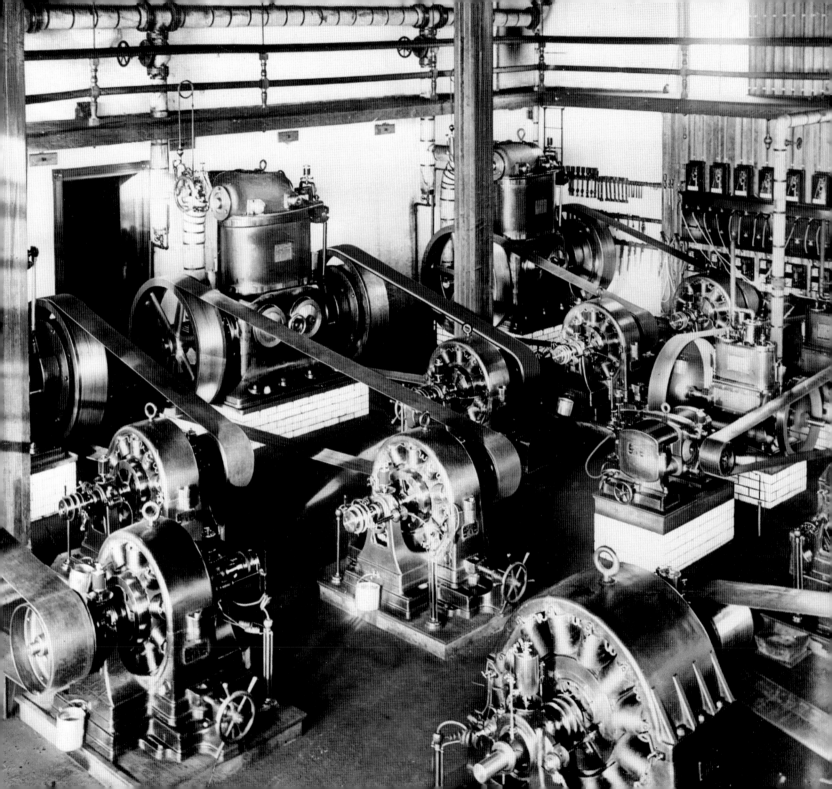

NIKOLA TESLA

Born in 1856 in Croatia, Nikola Tesla showed early signs of genius. He could do calculus in his head, making his teachers think he was cheating. Although his father wanted him to become a priest, Tesla was far more interested in math and science. He studied engineering at the Polytechnic School in Austria, where he became fascinated by electricity, particularly the idea of using alternating current. Tesla could not find European investors to support his idea to build an AC motor and decided to move to the United States at age 28. He did not like what he saw. He called New York City "rough and unattractive" and said "[America] is a century behind Europe in civilization."[5] Nonetheless, his new home introduced him to an investor who saw the potential in his idea: George Westinghouse. Westinghouse offered Tesla so much money to use Tesla's AC motor that he later realized it would bankrupt his company. Tesla was so grateful for Westinghouse's support that he tore up the contract, keeping Westinghouse in business.

AC needed a different type of motor. That's where Nikola Tesla could help. He was developing just such a machine. When Westinghouse heard about it, he struck a deal with Tesla in 1888 to use his invention. Even the directors of Edison's own company overrode his opinion and embraced the technology. Today, AC remains the standard method of delivery.

Nikola Tesla advanced the AC method of delivering electricity.

CHAPTER 5

ELECTRIC LIGHTS SPREAD

P aul de Rousiers, a French visitor to a small settlement in the Oklahoma Territory in 1891, observed the bright arc lights that shone over the streets at night. The lights served no practical purpose the visitor could see—people were home in the evening and did not need them. The man concluded the townspeople could see the lights from the windows of their houses and the illumination made residents feel "confident" about the future.[1] Electricity was a symbol of a progressive society, so towns and cities across the United States that could afford electric light eagerly sought it to demonstrate their modern ways.

The use of electricity in the United States spread quickly, lighting a levee in New Orleans, Louisiana, in the 1880s.

CHRISTMAS LIGHTS

Decorating Christmas trees is an old tradition. Before electric lights were invented, people sometimes illuminated their trees with candles. While pretty, this practice was unreliable, messy, and dangerous. A better solution lay in electric lights. Edward H. Johnson, an associate of Edison, is credited with being the first person to use electric Christmas tree lights. In 1882, he decorated his tree with approximately 80 lights in red, white, and blue. General Electric started offering them to the public around the turn of the century. Some Christmas lights used bulbs made of colored glass, while others were painted on the outside. The glass could also be blown into a variety of figures, including flowers, fruit, and holiday figures. Early lights were expensive, costing the equivalent of approximately $300 in 2015 for a single string.[2]

Taking Them to the Streets

Such strong lights might have been overkill in a small settlement, but they were practical in places with larger populations and the crime that came with them. During the second half of the 1800s, as industrialization continued, people worked extremely long hours, often leaving work after the sun had set. Walking home in the dark could be dangerous, especially for women. Criminals could easily hide in the flickering shadows of gaslights or escape down darkened alleys.

Gas lighting was not great at preventing crime. The gas supply could simply be shut off by would-be criminals. Even when they burned, gaslights provided halos of weak, yellowy light that were not nearly as powerful as the piercing beams of electric arc lights. Lighting streets, parks, and other public areas with electric lights essentially reclaimed large spaces for innocent citizens. As James Hodges, the mayor of Baltimore, Maryland, noted in 1886, "An electric light is a nocturnal joy to an honest man, but a scarecrow to a thief."[3]

Helping keep people safe might have been the electric light's most noble contribution. It also had other benefits. Lights left on inside shops discouraged thieves from breaking in, for example. One creative use was demonstrated in Chicago, Illinois, in 1886. The city was notorious for its fraudulent elections, so an official arranged for the polls to be brightly lit to deter ballot stuffers and thugs who might try to intimidate voters.

Up All Night

People in the late 1800s were unaccustomed to electric light and enchanted by its bright, steady glow. Light attracted people, and businesses soon saw the smart economics in investing in electric light to draw customers. Electric light cracked open the night, creating far more hours for people to amuse themselves—and to spend money doing it. Because light was more readily available in urban areas than in the country, rural residents flocked to the city to take in the nightlife there. Historian Ernest Freeberg noted, "[Electric light] really created what we think of as the modern city."[4]

Carnivals and fairs were among the first to drape their attractions in electric lighting. Large arenas installed lights so they could hold nighttime sporting events. Restaurants stayed open late.

A TRICK OF THE LIGHT

In 1881, London's Savoy Theatre became the first theater to install electric lighting. To reassure the audience that the electric lights were not a fire hazard, legendary theater producer D'Oyly Carte went on stage and gave his own performance. He wrapped a piece of muslin, which could easily catch fire, around a lit light bulb and then broke the bulb with a hammer. The light instantly went out and Carte displayed the muslin, which was free of burns, to the audience to prove electricity was safe.

Of course, nightlife existed before electricity—gaslights lit the streets and the insides of buildings. But the smoky, noxious gas lamps sucked oxygen and pumped out heat. In indoor spaces, people would sometimes end up overheated and sick. Worse, the open flames of gaslights presented a constant danger. Theaters were especially vulnerable to such disasters. Not only were gas lamps used for general illumination, but the performances themselves used lighting for dramatic effects. The errant swish of a curtain or dress could quickly cause a fire. Two hundred people were killed when a fire broke out at the Opera Comique theater in Paris, France, in 1887.[5] Afterward, Paris authorities gave theaters three months to replace their gas lighting with electric lighting.

The first electric lights used in theaters were the harsh, bright arc lights. Though they were brighter and safer, they had drawbacks. The costumes, sets, and makeup that could approximate reality in dim gas lighting looked fake in the brilliant glare of arc lighting.

The wife of businessman Cornelius Vanderbilt impressed New York partygoers at an 1883 ball dressed as electric light, wearing a yellow satin dress sequined with tiny, battery-powered light bulbs.

Incandescent lights were a big improvement. Lighting and costume designers seized on the possibilities offered by this flexible source of light, learning how to use colored filters and direct the beams to create various effects.

Changing Work Patterns

The light bulb also changed work, perhaps more than any other facet of life. The brighter light made operating complicated machinery safer, and workers were less likely to go home with gas-induced headaches. In addition, the quality of light offered by the incandescent bulb was superior to previous forms of light. Incandescent lights more clearly represented colors, which was important in industries such as

PROPOSED INTRODUCTION
OF THE
ELECTRIC LIGHT IN CENTRAL PARK.

BEFORE THE INTRODUCTION OF THE ELECTRIC LIGHT.

AFTER THE INTRODUCTION OF THE ELECTRIC LIGHT.
[NOT EDISON'S.]

LOVERS WHO IMAGINE THE SHADOW CONCEALS THEM
FROM VULGAR GAZE.

A proposal for lights in New York's Central Park illustrates how the addition of light will keep away romantic couples.

textiles and printing. Blue looked like blue, not a shade of green produced by the yellow tint of gaslight.

Electric lights also made working longer hours possible. Machinery was an expensive investment, and industrialists saw that it made economic sense to keep it running as much as possible. Eventually, the workday expanded to 24 hours with the addition of a night shift. Labor unions took up the issue of constant work, protesting night work and the effect it had of prolonging an already long day. Nonetheless, production of goods increased, setting the stage for an economy that operates nonstop and dominates the world today.

While electric light brought its own issues, it certainly improved on its predecessors. Most workers were more than happy to be rid of gas lighting. One editor at a Washington, DC, newspaper found numerous unflattering adjectives for the hated gas lighting. After the paper switched to electric light, he noted smugly, "The smoky-yellow glare of the villainous fluid which the gas company kindly permits to ooze through its kerosene-tar clogged pipes only exists in memory."[6]

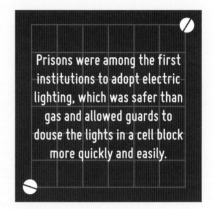

Prisons were among the first institutions to adopt electric lighting, which was safer than gas and allowed guards to douse the lights in a cell block more quickly and easily.

New Technologies

Incandescent bulbs get most of the credit for the lighting revolution, but they were only one lighting technology. As early as the 1850s, scientists experimented with gas discharge lamps. Rather than using an electrified filament, discharge lamps work by passing electricity through a gas or vapor. With some substances, such as neon, the electric current causes the gas to glow. With other gases, the release of electrons creates ultraviolet light, which is invisible. Next, the ultraviolet light reacts with substances called phosphors, which are painted on the inside of the tube. In a process known as fluorescence, the phosphors absorb the ultraviolet light and convert it into visible light. Fluorescent lights, which are common today, are a type of gas discharge lamp.

GEISSLER TUBES

In the 1850s, the German glassblower Heinrich Geissler developed an effective vacuum pump for emptying glass bulbs. He then filled them with a gas such as neon and sealed metal electrodes inside. When an electric current passed through the neon, it emitted a bright light. Geissler formed his tubes into elaborate shapes, incorporating twists and spirals to make them attractive works of art. His tubes were the forerunners of modern neon lights.

Daniel McFarlan Moore, an Edison researcher in the early 1890s, remarked to his boss that he hoped to make a light that resembled natural daylight even better than the incandescent bulb. Moore ultimately left Edison's company and set up his own, the Moore Electric Company, in 1894. He began producing gas discharge lamps filled with nitrogen, carbon dioxide, and later neon. Edison continued working on fluorescent technology and applied for his first patent on an electric fluorescent lamp two years later, in 1896.

Another pioneer in fluorescent lighting in the late 1890s was Peter Cooper Hewitt. He developed a mercury vapor lamp, which lit up when an electric current passed through the gas. The lamps gave off much more light than a traditional incandescent bulb. Unfortunately, the color was an unappealing bluish-green that most people did not want in their homes. However, in 1898, he achieved success with the bulb, creating the first of its kind to produce a good color of light.

These fluorescent lights were more efficient than incandescent lights, releasing more of their energy as light instead of heat. Their color, however, had a bluish tint, rather than the warm yellow of an incandescent light. They were also more difficult to install and operate. Nonetheless, these inventors did find a niche for their lights in black-and-white photography and in industrial settings.

Fluorescents were not able to supplant incandescent lighting, but their development posed a challenge to the incandescent bulb and spurred improvements to that type of bulb. As the turn of the century brought more widespread electric light, it got better and cheaper.

Peter Cooper Hewitt poses with one of his light bulbs in the early 1900s.

SIGNS OF
THE TIME

B y the 1890s, New York's Broadway was so ablaze with electric lights that it was called the "Great White Way," though the lights glowed in colors more than white.[7] In fact, they were a rainbow of hues that flashed on and off, advertising products from soap to soup. Signs could be visible for miles, and some were downright garish, at least according to the critics of a 45-foot-long (14 m) pickle, lit with green lights, that advertised the Heinz Company.[8]

Broadway lights circa 1915 include a kitten playing with string.

Lights on Broadway circa 1910 advertise alcohol, cigarettes, and theaters.

As signs got more sophisticated and creative, the lights were timed to create the illusion of movement. A technician operated some of the first signs, keeping everything running at the right time. The signs became automated as they got more complicated.

One elaborate display showed a 30-second chariot race from the days of ancient Rome, re-creating the running of the horses, the turning

Broadway's Times Square glows with electric advertisements in 1960.

of the chariot wheels, and the intent drivers cracking their whips to spur on the horses. Drivers' clothing flapped in the wind, dust swirled from the track, and the horses' manes swished realistically in the air. The sign was huge, stretching 72 feet (22 m) high—seven stories—and 90 feet (27 m) wide.[9] The sign required 20,000 light bulbs that flashed 2,500 times each minute, as well as 70,000 connections over almost 100 miles (160 km) of wire.[10] The spectacle drew such large crowds that a special police detail was dispatched just to keep the traffic moving. The sign was paid for by advertisers eager to put their names atop the screen.

Some people lamented the loss of quiet and simple streets, but advertisers knew electric signs caught people's attention best in the dark, a great time of day for advertising. As one advocate pointed out, "It takes [a man] in the best part of the day, when he has shaken off business affairs and is seeking recreation. He is in the best possible mood for persuasion."[11] More than large department stores and corporations cashed in on electric-light advertising and promotion. In New York City, even some churches erected electric signs to help them stand out among all the signs for commercial ventures.

Today, lights shine night and day on Broadway, advertising products and productions.

CHAPTER 6

THE MEANING OF LIGHT

T he war of the currents was fought across the entire landscape of the United States, but there was a much smaller battle zone as well: the inside of the light bulb itself. There might not have been much room inside a light bulb, but there was a lot of room for improvement.

Building a Better Bulb

Most early bulbs used carbon in their filaments. Carbon, however, had to be burned at a relatively low temperature. When it was burned at higher temperatures, the carbon would coat the inside

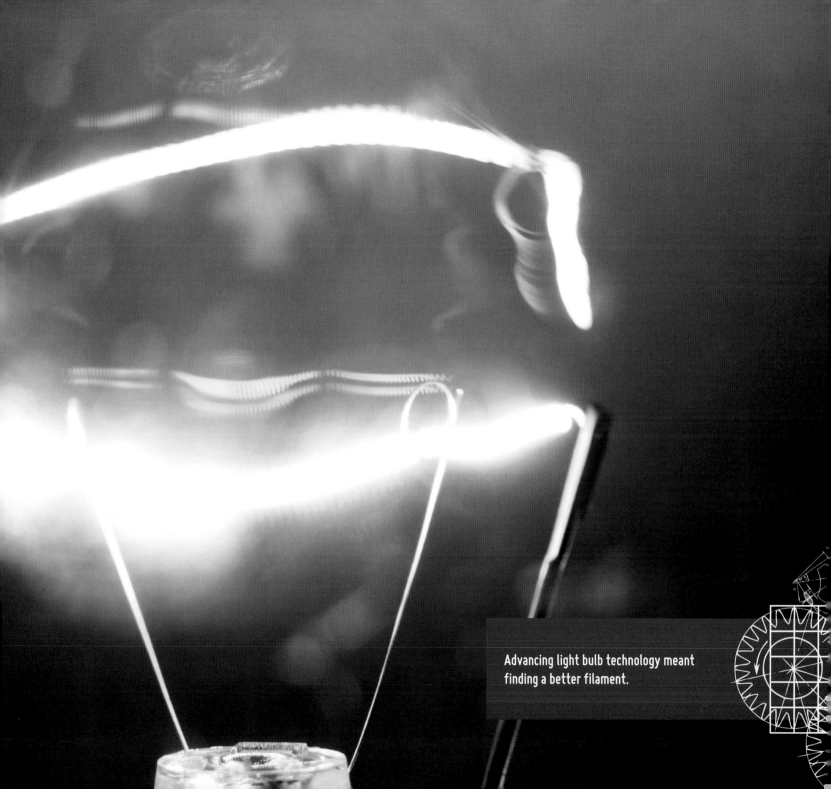

Advancing light bulb technology meant finding a better filament.

of the bulb with a black, sooty residue. In addition, inventors wanted a filament that would require less energy and last longer than carbon.

Carl Auer van Welsbach, an Austrian, experimented with filaments made from osmium, a type of metal. Osmium proved better than carbon in terms of light output, but these filaments broke easily and were hard to manufacture. Next, inventors such as the Germans Werner von Bolton and Otto Feuerlien tried the metal tantalum. It was not as efficient as osmium in terms of light output, but the material was sturdier. Then, several European inventors turned to tungsten in 1904. It had the highest melting point of the metals and made a brighter light, but tungsten was difficult to work with because it could not be twisted or bent. But in 1909, GE researcher William Coolidge developed a method to heat the tungsten and make it easier to shape. That made it a viable filament option. Soon after, chemist Irving Langmuir further improved light bulbs by introducing a tightly coiled tungsten filament. This increased the surface area of the metal and created more light. Langmuir also filled the bulb with a mix of nitrogen and argon, which made the filament last longer.

Sleepless Nights

Improved lighting affected people in a perhaps unexpected way. There are only so many hours in the day, and as work and play hours got longer, nights got shorter. Sleep was the main victim. In 2012, as David Randall wrote of the shift in *Dreamland: Adventures in the Strange Science of Sleep*, "Sleep took a backseat to nightlife and other more important priorities, and it has never regained its former place."[1]

Not only did extended work and play hours compete with the relatively dull activity of sleep, but so did the mere presence of light itself. The human body operates according to an internal timetable called the circadian clock. This system regulates when the body naturally understands it is time to sleep or time to wake up. It developed in response to natural light patterns—that is, day and night. With artificial sunlight now able to stream into virtually every place at every time, people's bodies became "confused" and fought to stay awake even though they desperately needed sleep. Although the effects of sleep deprivation were not well understood in the early 1900s, studies since then have shown a habitual lack of sleep can contribute to myriad health problems, including depression, obesity, and heart disease.

THE BIRDS AND THE BULBS

In the early days of electric lighting, reports abounded of birds being drawn into artificially lit areas and buildings, often with fatal consequences. Flocks of migrating ducks and geese became disoriented and sometimes flew into lights. Some were electrocuted. One sensational story involved a flock of ducks colliding with a brightly lit steamship. One reporter noted, "Country ducks are not familiar with Edison's invention."[2] Bats and insects were also affected. Although such stories are no longer considered newsworthy, the deaths have not ended. Scientists estimate hundreds of millions of birds still crash into lighted buildings each year.

LIVING BY THE DARK AND LIGHT OF THE BROOKLYN BRIDGE

When New York City's Brooklyn Bridge was completed in the 1880s, the massive structure put the tenement apartments at its base constantly in shadow. One family saw sunlight only at noon until workers installed electric arc lights to light the bridge at night. Those lights also shone through apartment windows all night. In response, the tenants simply reversed their pattern of living, working at night when they could see and sleeping during the day. One apartment resident explained, "We were all glad enough to have the electric light shine into our rooms, though it's blinding and sort of hard, and we would like to see the sun once in a while. But I go out for that."[3] Another tenant said, "We've light enough now, thank God, an' one that'll stay."[4]

The Science of Seeing

Longer days and shorter nights were an obvious result of electric lighting, but a more subtle issue concerned how the light really affected people—not the hours, but the actual light itself. Despite the fact that electric light was commonplace by the 1920s and 1930s, its effects were still not well understood. Scientists and sociologists had vague notions that light improved productivity, but they were not quite clear how. The general thinking followed the idea that more is better. Lighting companies were eager to increase profits, so they often suggested customers purchase far more lights than were actually needed for a given space.

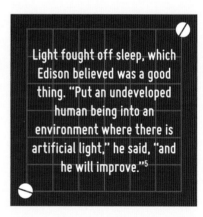

Light fought off sleep, which Edison believed was a good thing. "Put an undeveloped human being into an environment where there is artificial light," he said, "and he will improve."[5]

At General Electric, engineer Matthew Luckiesh studied the effects of lighting in the workplace. He concluded that the amount and quality of light had a tremendous effect on workers, raising productivity, keeping the workplace safer, and contributing to overall health and morale. In fact, Luckiesh contended that artificial light could, and should, replace natural light. Windows, he said, wasted space in buildings. They added cost because they were more expensive than solid walls, plus they required washing. Artificial light was a cheaper, easier, and preferable solution. "This is in reality the age of artificial light, for mankind has not only become independent of daylight in certain respects, but has improved upon natural light," Luckiesh wrote in a book on the subject. "The controllability of artificial light makes it superior to natural light in many ways. [It] has numerous advantages over light which has been furnished by the Creator."[6]

THE HAWTHORNE EXPERIMENTS

In the 1920s, a series of experiments conducted at the Hawthorne plant of the Western Electric Company aimed to show the connections between light and work productivity. Although subjects in the study performed tasks under very different lighting conditions, their productivity showed little variation. Researchers concluded that the amount of light was largely unimportant to workers and their performance depended on social factors, such as how much interaction they had with other people.

To an extent, more detailed tasks did require better lighting. After a certain threshold was reached, however, more light did not necessarily mean better performance. In some cases, it actually proved to be a detriment, as bright lights were glaring and uncomfortable. In addition, workers missed the psychological comfort of being able to look out a window. Yet, as electric lights became more prevalent in the late 1800s and early 1900s, some factories and schools embraced them entirely. These buildings, constructed without any windows, sacrificed natural light altogether.

Illumination Engineers

In the early 1900s, few people understood that light could be used to enhance a space, not just brighten it. Fewer still had any idea how to achieve that goal. Most balked at the idea of muting a light bulb's power with a lampshade. Instead, they subscribed to the notion that more light was preferable and neglected to take into account the quality or effects of the light.

But as artificial light spread, people grappled with the subtleties of how light could be used, and—perhaps more important—how it should be used. Lighting was one thing, but illumination was quite another. Lighting focused on the mundane equipment of lamps and bulbs, while illumination covered a more complex array of problems and possibilities. It embraced the overall effect of lights and their placement on an entire area.

At first, lighting was tacked on to existing streets and structures, but as towns grew and new buildings developed, people incorporated lighting into their designs at the outset. And rather than being only about the numbers—that

An early street lamp provides outdoor light in Pennsylvania circa 1900.

is, how many bulbs—lighting became more about where lights were placed, how they were arranged to contribute to the overall building and city design, and the character of the light produced.

By 1906, the Illuminating Engineering Society, a professional organization, formed. Its members focused on the various ways lighting could be used in architecture and civic planning. The organization's position was that civilians could not hope to understand the many variations and factors that went into such decisions; a professional was necessary to navigate this new field.

These illumination engineers had plenty of work in front of them. The first decades of the 1900s saw an explosion of light across the country, penetrating more and more places and bringing even the most remote areas under the shining umbrella of electric light.

CITY BEAUTIFUL

In the late 1800s, towns and cities were not planned out. Rather, people created buildings and streets as needed. The results were often haphazard and ugly. American architect Daniel Burnham helped change that. At the 1893 World's Fair, in Chicago, Burnham created a huge model city of 150 buildings as the centerpiece attraction. His "White City" was a collection of tall, white-sided buildings illuminated with electric lights. His model city later inspired the designs in real ones, including Washington, DC, and San Francisco, California. His exhibition helped launch the City Beautiful Movement, an effort to create beauty and order in US cities.

A young woman working in a light bulb factory circa 1910 seals bulbs.

CHAPTER 7

LIGHTING
THE WAY

Despite its popularity, electricity took a while to become widespread. In general, businesses got it first. Residences got electricity later because few people could afford to have their homes rewired for the new technology. In 1910, nearly 30 years after Edison opened his Pearl Street Station in New York, only approximately 15 percent of US homes had electricity.[1] But that was about to change.

Growing the Grid

Electric companies, eager to increase market share, began aggressively pushing their products. They also worked to improve

A farmer stands next to power lines that brought electricity to people living beyond big cities.

the technology. Larger generating stations and better equipment lowered prices and made electricity affordable to more people. By 1930, electricity had reached approximately 70 percent of the public, although it was still mostly in urban and suburban areas.[2] Rural America was still waiting. Ironically, it took an economic crisis to help bring the countryside a more modern way of life.

The US stock market crashed in 1929, plunging the nation and much of the world into the Great Depression, which lasted for the next decade. President Franklin D. Roosevelt's principal goal during this time was to create jobs, and he instituted his sweeping New Deal program to do just that. Under the New Deal, the government launched many federal agencies and programs to employ people and improve the nation's infrastructure at the same time.

In 1935, the US government established the Rural Electrification Administration (REA). The agency provided federal money to run electric lines to the millions of Americans who lived in the country. Without electricity, many of these residents were living the way people had 50 years earlier.

Over the next two years, the agency ran approximately 73,000 miles (117,000 km) of electric lines, finally bringing lights to more than 300,000 farms.[3] Adding electricity, and the light that came with it, was a cause for celebration. Officials spoke about progress and modernity. In many cases, the proceedings included a ceremonial funeral for the old ways, with a gas or oil lamp being buried in the ground.

By 1942, approximately 40 percent of the US countryside was wired for electricity, although progress dropped during World War II (1939–1945) as money and resources went to the war effort.[4] After the war, the REA stepped up its efforts once again, and by the 1950s, most US homes had electricity.

Blackouts

Electricity was spreading fast, and it had some growing pains. Lights went out frequently. They burned out, the electric circuit shorted out, or the power station failed. In the first half of the 1900s, the grid was not the national network it is today. Local stations supplied most electricity. For people accustomed to living without electric light, the loss of light was just a temporary return to an earlier time. When the power went out, people simply pulled out their flashlights or lit candles and waited for it to come back on. Fortunately, when a station went down, it did not ripple down the line to knock out neighboring stations, so relatively few people were affected at any one time.

By the mid-1900s, though, the standard had changed. Light and electricity had become expected and necessary. Power outages could be a major inconvenience, and possibly worse. The reliance on electric light meant that natural

FLIP THE SWITCH FOR BETTER SLEEP

Some of the REA's new customers did not understand the new technology. One complained that the light was keeping her awake at night. She got a response explaining what a light switch was and where to find it.

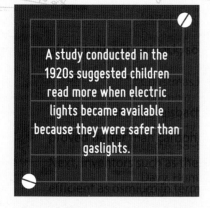

A study conducted in the 1920s suggested children read more when electric lights became available because they were safer than gaslights.

light often had been relegated to something that was an extra, not a requirement, and some factories, schools, and shopping malls had no windows at all. In a blackout, people in these buildings would be plunged into utter darkness, making it difficult for them to get out. In addition, the grid had become a complex maze of wires and stations connecting vast regions, so far more people were affected during power outages.

On November 9, 1965, a major portion of the US electric grid failed in the Northeast, plunging millions of customers into darkness. It started with a faulty circuit breaker. At approximately 5:30 p.m., the amount of power on the circuit breaker's line increased. The circuit breaker incorrectly interpreted the increase to mean the line was overloaded, and it automatically shut down the line. The power that was on that line moved to other lines. That increase meant those lines really were carrying too much, so they shut down as well. Within seconds, the delicate balance became upset and electricity ceased to flow. The lights went out across all of New York and most of New England, and they stayed that way for almost 13 hours. Thousands of people were trapped wherever they happened to be—in a store if they were lucky, in a subway car or elevator if they were not. Some enterprising efforts allowed life to limp along. At New York's LaGuardia Airport, power from a water pump was commandeered to light a runway. Doctors used flashlights and candles to attend to their duties. Less critical activities continued as well.

Passengers stranded while riding New York's subway when the 1965 blackout hit made their way through the tunnels on foot.

The nation has experienced several major blackouts since then, and while the grid always recovers, even temporary losses of electricity can cause panic, injuries, and death and cost billions of dollars. Sometimes, rather than a total blackout, the thirst for power can tax the grid's capabilities and stifle the amount of available electricity, causing a brownout. In a brownout, lights do not go out but dim as the power is spread too thin because there is not enough to go around at full capacity.

More Improvements

Finding more energy-efficient ways of using electricity was becoming a priority by the mid-1900s. Consumers started scrutinizing their power use, and government and industry began looking for ways to cut back. By this time, researchers were experimenting with new forms of lighting, including halogen lights, compact fluorescent lights (CFLs), and light-emitting diodes (LEDs).

A variation on the incandescent light bulb is the halogen light, which Elmer Fridrich and Emmett Wiley developed at General Electric in 1955. Halogen lamps operate just as an incandescent light does, with a glowing filament. The bulb, however, is filled with a halogen gas, such as chlorine, iodine, or bromine. In a regular incandescent bulb, the tungsten filament vaporizes over time. The tungsten collects on the inside of the bulb, turning it black. Eventually, the filament wears out and becomes too thin to burn. In a halogen light, however, the gas reacts with the tungsten so the tungsten does not collect on the inside of the bulb, and some of the tungsten is deposited back onto the filament, which makes it last longer. Halogen bulbs do have disadvantages, however. They cost more than regular incandescent bulbs, and they burn extremely hot and can sometimes explode. In addition, they are difficult to handle because the oils from human skin can disrupt the performance of the bulb.

Other improvements came with fluorescent lights, which are more efficient than incandescent bulbs and became widely used in offices, industrial settings, and countless basements and garages. Their shape, however, was long and thin, which made them inconvenient to stick in bedside lamps and ugly to hang from the ceiling. They also took a while to light up and tended to flicker once they did. Plus, most people preferred the softer yellow light of incandescents to the unflattering bluish tint of fluorescents. But though fluorescents were more efficient and cheaper in the long run, the overall cost of light was low enough that expense was not a primary concern for most people.

LUMENS AND WATTS

Light output is measured in units called lumens, which measure the brightness, or amount of light a bulb gives off. The amount of power consumed by the light is measured in watts. Typically, higher wattage bulbs are also brighter. Energy-efficient bulbs, however, use less power to produce the same amount of light. For example, a standard 60-watt incandescent bulb could give off roughly 800 lumens, while a CFL or LED light can put out the same amount of lumens using approximately 13 watts.[5]

PLAYING WITH LIGHT

In 1963, the Kenner Company introduced a new toy: the Easy Bake Oven. Its power source was a single light bulb. Even though baking requires heat, not light, the inefficient incandescent light bulb was a perfect energy source because most of its energy, approximately 90 percent, came out as heat.[6] The toy was enormously popular. Kenner sold 500,000 ovens the first year and 30 million by its fiftieth anniversary in 2013.[7] As incandescent light bulbs are being phased out, however, the toy ovens no longer use them. In 2011, they began operating with a heating element similar to those used in regular ovens. Lite-Brite, another popular toy introduced in 1967, lets children create pictures using colored pegs that are illuminated by a light bulb.

The 1970s, however, brought an energy crisis when an oil embargo in the Middle East caused gasoline prices to skyrocket and plunged the United States and other countries into an economic recession. The event also highlighted the fact that Americans were consuming energy at alarming rates.

With conservation and efficiency becoming more urgent, researchers at various lighting companies revisited the issue of fluorescents. In 1976, GE researcher Edward E. Hammer found a way to twist the light bulb into a spiral shape. Stick a socket on the end, and these CFLs could be adapted to the traditional screw base used by incandescent bulbs. The first mass-produced CFL bulb with a screw base came out in 1980. But issues remained. Often, they were still too large to fit inside the glass covering. And at a cost of approximately $30 each, they were expensive. Over time, prices came down and the bulbs got smaller. In addition, the technology improved so the lights lost their annoying flicker and came on instantly, and the color more closely

Adding a screw base to Edward E. Hammer's twisted fluorescent bulb advanced bulb technology to make CFLs a viable replacement for incandescent bulbs.

approximated the warmer light of an incandescent bulb. CFLs gained in popularity in the late 1990s and early 2000s but are becoming less popular as a newer technology penetrates the market: LEDs.

IN A FLASH

Photographers used to burn chemicals such as magnesium to produce a strong light to illuminate their pictures. But this flash powder produced a lot of smoke and could be dangerous. Subsequent experiments burned substances such as magnesium or aluminum inside a glass bulb. The first true flashbulbs produced a short-lived but bright light, but they were big and bulky, the size of a standard light bulb, and they were only used once. Over time, they got smaller and could be fitted directly onto cameras. Today, most cameras have a built-in flash.

CHAPTER 8

ELECTRIC LIGHT
TODAY

In the 2010s, lights come in a variety of technologies, from incandescent to fluorescent to LED. In this new light landscape, Edison's light bulb has become antiquated, but the changes it brought are firmly rooted in the lives of billions of people.

Effect on Industries

Flexibility was vital to the success of the electric light. It was easy and portable, and it could go far more places than the cumbersome gaslights of the previous era. Even when a wired power source was unavailable, electric lights could obtain power from batteries. Battery technology advanced hand in hand with electricity, and

Since Edison perfected his incandescent bulb, inventors have continuously worked to improve electric light bulbs.

while batteries were not—and still are not—powerful enough to replace hard wiring, they have proved invaluable for temporary use, particularly in remote locations.

The advent of electric light allowed people to explore the darkest places on the planet, deep underground and miles below the surface of the sea. In the 1800s, miners literally played with fire when they descended into the earth with gas lamps, whose open flames could ignite the natural gases trapped under the ground and cause an explosion. Electric lamps mounted on their helmets removed this danger. In ocean depths, only electricity is suitable for shining light into the dark crevasses of underwater formations to see what might live there.

Electric light has helped with exploration well beyond Earth. The complete blackness of space becomes visible only through the glow of electric light, as there is no atmosphere to support light produced from gas or oil.

Back on solid ground, medicine was one of the greatest beneficiaries of electric lights. Brighter, safer lighting made delicate operations easier to perform, and they could be performed at any time of day. In some cases, light itself became the medicine, as an entire specialized field of light therapeutics arose. While the specifics were not well understood in the early 1900s, empirical evidence showed the very real need for exposure to light. People with the condition seasonal affective disorder (SAD) feel more depressed in the winter because of the relative lack of sunshine.

Special lights help people with seasonal affective disorder get through the challenging winter months.

Stepping outside for a while may help, but when that is not practical, many SAD sufferers spend time in front of an electric light box to soak up artificial—but still helpful—rays.

Too Much and Not Enough

When electric lighting first became available, it was both desired and feared. As it spread slowly from offices to homes and from cities to the country, it became a symbol of progress, often dividing the haves from the have-nots. Those who could afford electric lighting got it. Those who could not afford it made do with more primitive forms of lighting. Meanwhile, the increased amount of light drew critics who believed artificial light destroyed the purity of the natural world and disrupted age-old rhythms of life.

More than 100 years later, the arguments have not changed. While almost everyone in the developed world has reliable access to electricity, large parts of the developing world still do not. Approximately 1 billion people living in poor and remote regions in Africa, Asia, India, and elsewhere still rely on candles and kerosene lamps for much of their lighting.[1] In some places, this severely cuts into a family's finances, as almost one-third of a family's income can be spent on buying

In 2010, the US Department of Energy estimated the number of 60-watt incandescent light bulbs in use in the United States at approximately 971 million.[2]

kerosene.[3] In addition, the smoke and fumes from kerosene are bad for people's health.

Several charitable organizations are devoted to bringing electricity and light to those who do not have it. Some areas are bypassing the incandescent bulb altogether, choosing instead to use LEDs because they require less power than incandescent and fluorescent bulbs. LED technology also is particularly compatible with solar-generated electricity, which is a natural choice in remote areas where stringing complex wiring or hauling in bulky generators is difficult.

On the downside, light can dominate every hour of every day. Constant activity has increased productivity to a point, but it comes with costs. Sleep deprivation makes workers less productive, and in the extreme can be a safety hazard. Every year, stories emerge about truckers who fall asleep on the road after pushing themselves for too many hours or doctors who make fatal mistakes after being on duty for long stretches.

THE SOLAR SUITCASE

When California doctor Laura Stachel was visiting Nigeria in 2008, the power went out during an emergency Caesarean section, a way of delivering a baby that requires surgery. She pulled out a flashlight and finished the procedure. Later, she realized her patient had been lucky. For many others, an operation would simply have had to wait. Sometimes, people died for the very simple reason of having no available light. Stachel went on to design a solar suitcase, a suitcase equipped with solar panels, solar-powered LEDs, and other equipment designed to provide power during an emergency.

THE MYSTERY CLOUD

A 1994 earthquake in Los Angeles, California, knocked out power to much of the city. In the unfamiliar darkness, people looked up into the sky and saw a strange sight. Some called authorities to report the "giant, silvery cloud" overhead.[5] Doomsday was not at hand. The quake had not released dangerous gases into the atmosphere. What people were seeing had, in fact, been there far longer than Earth itself. It was the Milky Way, the band of stars that make up the galaxy, but the city's residents had not been able to see it through the lights of the city.

Electric light has also changed the physical landscape. In large cities, complete darkness no longer exists. Even at night, electric light produces a low-level illumination that is impossible to escape. The natural night sky has become largely invisible and a curiosity for those who live in densely populated and heavily lit areas. Some astronomers grumble about the pervasiveness of light pollution, which occurs when artificial light increases the brightness of the night sky and limits visibility of the night sky. They point out that 99 percent of Americans live in areas so polluted by light that studying the stars is difficult, if not impossible.[4] Some people are fighting back. In 1988, the International Dark-Sky Association formed to limit light pollution. Members work with lighting companies to encourage technology that helps lights aim down instead of up into the sky and support citizens in passing local laws that limit light pollution.

The glow of cities such as Los Angeles causes light pollution that keeps people from seeing the night sky fully.

After 100 years of electric lighting and the emergence of better bulbs, Edison's bulb remains popular.

More Than a Century of Light

The year 1929 marked the fiftieth anniversary of Edison's light bulb, and on October 21 President Herbert Hoover gave a speech to celebrate the occasion. Hoover spoke about the effects of the invention:

> *And by all its multiple uses, it has lengthened the hours of our active lives, decreased our fears, replaced the dark with good cheer, increased our safety, decreased our toil, and enabled us to read the type in the telephone book. It has become the friend of man and child.*[6]

Decades have elapsed since Hoover's words, yet their basic message still applies. The light bulb created demands no one envisioned at first. It created a market for electricity, which in turn created markets for more machines and applications. Today, the process has come full circle. As new electric gadgets appear on store shelves, entire industries are devoted to finding alternative ways to produce the electricity on which the world depends. Light from the first electric light bulbs was limited, but it soon became vital for work and play alike. Those bulbs lit the path to the future, changing the way society functions. The electric light bulb led the way to the electric advances the world relies on and enjoys today and will continue to use and enjoy tomorrow.

THE EDISON BULB

When Thomas Edison first began manufacturing light bulbs, they looked different from the common bulbs of today. The glass was transparent, and the filaments inside emitted a soft amber glow. This retro design is experiencing a resurgence, and replicas of Edison's original bulbs can be purchased today and are popular with decorators who want to achieve a vintage look. As architect David Rockwell noted, "It's the closest electric thing to an open flame. It's like a hearth."[7]

THE NEXT GENERATION: LED LIGHTS

I n a world concerned with energy conservation, the inefficient incandescent light bulb is nearing the end of its useful life. The United States instituted new energy-efficiency requirements in 2007 the incandescent light bulb could not meet. Between 2012 and 2014, incandescents were gradually phased out in the United States, yoking the country's lighting future to alternatives such as LEDs.

In an LED, light is given off due to the movement of electrons within a semiconductor, a solid substance that allows partial electron flow, located in an LED chip. The diode has two electrodes connected by a wire that meet in the LED chip. One, the anode, has a positive charge and the other, the cathode, a negative one. As the electrons scurry back and forth trying to equalize the charges, they release light, a phenomenon known as electroluminescence. Compared with incandescents, LEDs require far less electricity, are six to seven times more efficient, and last approximately 25 times longer.[8]

LEDs were developed commercially in the 1960s. In 1962, GE researcher Nick Holonyak Jr. developed the first visible LEDs. These low-level red lights were only

Nick Holonyak Jr.,
inventor of the LED bulb

LEDs make a grouping of trees colorful and magical.

useful for small things, such as a clock display or the on-off light on a television. By the 1970s, the technology had gotten more sophisticated and developers had widened the color spectrum to include blue, green, and yellow. Today, colors can be combined to make white light—the most in-demand color for lighting.

The parts of an LED bulb

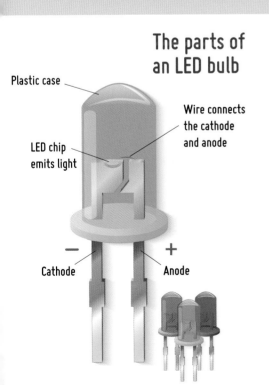

Plastic case

Wire connects the cathode and anode

LED chip emits light

− +

Cathode   Anode

LEDs have several benefits. They do not contain dangerous mercury gas and are tiny, only about the size of a pepper flake. They are also directional, meaning that rather than creating a halo of light all around a bulb, they send out a focused beam that makes them ideal for task lighting. LEDs are now used in traffic signal lights, parking garages, refrigerators, Christmas lights, and other places where long-lasting lights are needed. Some LEDs are tech-friendly. Users can control them with their smartphones and can program them to change their color based on the time, the weather, or even the winning team in a big game.

In 2012, the US Department of Energy estimated LEDs were saving the nation approximately $675 million a year over incandescent lights.[9] The downside was cost. At $10 or more per bulb, some customers found the cost a bit high, although the price was coming down.

DATE OF INVENTION

1879: Thomas Edison introduces the first practical incandescent light.

KEY PLAYERS

- Humphry Davy, an English inventor, experiments with both arc and incandescent lighting.

- Thomas Edison, an American inventor, creates the first practical incandescent light bulb and constructs a power system to serve customers.

- Nikola Tesla, a Serbian-American inventor, champions alternating current and, with the backing of American businessman George Westinghouse, establishes it as a viable alternative to Edison's direct current.

- Nick Holonyak Jr., a researcher at General Electric (GE), creates the first visible light using an LED.

- Edward Hammer, a GE researcher, devises a way to bend fluorescent tubes to create a compact fluorescent light (CFL).

KEY TECHNOLOGIES

- Arc lighting is the first form of electric light, produced by passing an electric current between two carbon or metal rods.

- Incandescent lighting is created by sending an electric current through a filament, heating it until it glows.

- Fluorescent lights, or gas discharge lamps, produce invisible light by passing an electric current through a gas or vapor and then convert it to visible light through a chemical reaction.

- LEDs use semiconductors to convert electricity into light.

EVOLUTION AND UPGRADES

After the introduction of Edison's practical incandescent bulb, researchers made several improvements to filaments and to the construction of bulbs. Over time, incandescents became cheaper and produced more and better-quality light. However, they are still extraordinarily inefficient in their energy use. CFLs and LEDs are far more energy-efficient than incandescents and last several times longer. Although more expensive, CFLs and LEDs are coming down in price as their technologies improve and consumer demand increases. These technologies will likely change the future of lighting, especially as incandescent lights are phased out of production.

IMPACT ON SOCIETY

Electric light bulbs are safer and brighter than the gas lighting that preceded them. Electric bulbs transformed industries that depend on better lighting, leading to longer workdays and influencing the growth of cities. The light bulb also spurred the development of the electricity industry as a whole, eventually bringing electricity to billions of people. Increased access to electricity created a market for numerous electric appliances, fundamentally changing how people live and work.

QUOTE

"After Edison, light and fire are always going to be separate."

—*David Nye, historian*

alternating current

A type of electricity, often referred to simply as AC, in which electrons flow in both directions.

ballot stuffer

Someone who cheats during an election by submitting more than the one vote per person that is allowed.

circadian clock

A system in the body that naturally responds to day and night patterns.

direct current

A type of electricity, often referred to simply as DC, in which electrons flow in a single direction.

electrode

Something used to conduct electricity.

electron

A negatively charged particle that is part of an atom.

embargo

The act of banning or denying the supply of a product.

filament

The part of an incandescent light bulb that glows when electricity passes through it.

fluorescent

A type of light that uses a substance to convert invisible light into visible light.

gas discharge

A type of lamp that passes an electric current through a gas or vapor and causes it to light up.

generator

A machine that converts mechanical energy into electrical energy.

incandescent

A type of light produced by heat.

infrastructure

The physical or organizational systems put in place to help a society operate.

patent

A permit issued by a government that grants a person the legal right to use or market an invention, technology, or process.

tenement

A type of inferior housing usually in a poorer neighborhood and occupied by people with low incomes.

vacuum

A space empty of any material, including air.

SELECTED BIBLIOGRAPHY

Freeberg, Ernest. *The Age of Edison: Electric Light and the Invention of Modern America*. New York: Penguin, 2013. Print.

Friedel, Robert, and Paul Israel. *Edison's Electric Light: Biography of an Invention*. New Brunswick, NJ: Rutgers UP, 1986. Print.

Jonnes, Jill. *Empires of Light: Edison, Tesla, Westinghouse, and the Race to Electrify the World*. New York: Random, 2003. Print.

Nye, David E. *Electrifying America: Social Meanings of a New Technology*. Cambridge, MA: MIT, 1990. Print.

FURTHER READINGS

Matthews, John R. *The Light Bulb*. New York: Franklin Watts, 2005. Print.

Parker, Steve. *Electricity*. London: DK, 2013. Print.

Pederson, Charles E. *Thomas Edison*. Minneapolis: Abdo, 2007. Print.

WEBSITES

To learn more about Essential Library of Inventions, visit **booklinks.abdopublishing.com**. These links are routinely monitored and updated to provide the most current information available.

FOR MORE INFORMATION

For more information on this subject, contact or visit the following organizations:

Edison Tech Center

136 North Broadway, Schenectady, NY 12305
518-372-8425
http://edisontechcenter.org

The Edison Tech Center produces videos and maintains a website on various topics related to engineering and sponsors occasional educational programs at their headquarters.

Lemelson Hall of Invention

National Museum of American History, Smithsonian Institution
14th St. and Constitution Ave. NW, Washington, DC 20001
202-633-1000
http://invention.si.edu/about/our-exhibits

An exhibit of American inventors includes Edison as well as Alexander Graham Bell and Samuel Morse.

Thomas Edison Center

Menlo Park, 37 Christie Street, Edison, NJ 08820
732-549-3299
http://www.menloparkmuseum.org

Visit the site's museum and explore exhibits to learn about Thomas Edison.

SOURCE NOTES

Chapter 1. Fourteen Hours

1. Vaclav Smil. *Creating the Twentieth Century*. Oxford, UK: Oxford UP, 2005. Print. 42–43.

2. Ernest Freeberg. *The Age of Edison: Electric Light and the Invention of Modern America*. New York: Penguin, 2013. Print. 35.

3. Jill Jonnes. *Empires of Light: Edison, Tesla, Westinghouse, and the Race to Electrify the World*. New York: Random House, 2003. Print. 63.

4. "Incandescent Lighting." *Edison Tech Center*. EdisonTech Center, 2010. Web. 1 Nov. 2014.

5. "Thomas Edison—Changing Our World Forever." *The Mark of a Leader*. N.p., n.d. Web. 30 Oct 2014.

Chapter 2. Out of the Dark

1. "Edison's Miracle of Light: Program Transcript." *PBS*. WGBH Educational Foundation, 2013. Web. 30 Oct. 2014.

Chapter 3. Power to the People

1. "Edison's Miracle of Light: Program Transcript." *PBS*. WGBH Educational Foundation, 2013. Web. 30 Oct. 2014.

2. Jill Jonnes. *Empires of Light: Edison, Tesla, Westinghouse, and the Race to Electrify the World*. New York: Random House, 2003. Print. 84.

3. Ibid. 71.

4. Ibid. 81.

5. Ibid. 84.

6. Vaclav Smil. *Creating the Twentieth Century*. Oxford, UK: Oxford UP, 2005. Print. 57.

7. Ibid. 58.

8. Ernest Freeberg. *The Age of Edison: Electric Light and the Invention of Modern America*. New York: Penguin, 2013. Print. 58.

9. Ibid. 61.

10. Ernest Freeberg. *The Age of Edison: Electric Light and the Invention of Modern America*. New York: Penguin, 2013. Print. 139.

Chapter 4. The Fight for Light

1. "Interviews—Paul Israel." *PBS*. Great Projects Film Company, Inc., 2002. Web. 8 Mar. 2015.

2. John Winthrop Hammond. *Men and Volts: The Story of General Electric*. Philadelphia, PA: Lippincott, 1941. Print. 47.

3. Alasdair Nairn. *Engines that Move Markets: Technology Investing from Railroads to the Internet and Beyond*. Hoboken, NJ: Wiley, 2002. Print. 126.

4. "Edison's Miracle of Light: Program Transcript." *PBS*. WGBH Educational Foundation, 2013. Web. 30 Oct. 2014.

5. "Tesla Life and Legacy—Coming to America." *PBS*. PBS, n.d. Web. 8 Mar. 2015.

Chapter 5. Electric Lights Spread

1. Paul de Rousiers. *American Life*. New York: Firmin-Didot, 1892. 132. *Archive.org*. n.p., n.d. Web. 8 Mar. 2015.

2. Chris Jacob. "Christmas Lights, the Brief and Strangely Interesting History of." *Gizmodo*. Gizmodo, 13 Dec. 2009. Web. 8 Nov. 2014.

3. *American Electrical Directory*. Star Iron Tower Co., 1886. *Google Book Search*. Web. 8 Mar. 2015.

4. Brooke Berger. "Many Minds Produced the Light that Illuminated America: Ernest Freeberg Shows the Light Bulb Reflected the Work of Many Inventors." *US News and World Report*. US News and World Report, 21 Mar. 2013. Web. 6 Nov. 2014.

5. Ernest Freeberg. *The Age of Edison: Electric Light and the Invention of Modern America*. New York: Penguin, 2013. Print. 109–110.

6. Ibid. 94.

7. David E. Nye. *Electrifying America: Social Meanings of a New Technology*. Cambridge, MA: MIT Press, 1990. Print. 244.

8. Ibid.

9. Ibid. 50–52.

10. Ibid. 53.

11. Ibid.

Chapter 6. The Meaning of Light

1. David K. Randall. *Dreamland: Adventures in the Strange Science of Sleep*. New York: Norton, 2012. Print. 39–40.

2. Ernest Freeberg. *The Age of Edison: Electric Light and the Invention of Modern America*. New York: Penguin, 2013. Print. 215–216.

3. Helen Campbell. *Darkness and Daylight*. Hartford, CT: A.D. Worthington, 1893. 273. *Google Book Search*. Web. 5 Nov. 2014.

4. Ibid. 272.

5. David K. Randall. *Dreamland: Adventures in the Strange Science of Sleep*. New York: Norton, 2012. Print. 40.

6. Matthew Luckiesh. *Artificial Light: Its Influence Upon Civilization*. New York: Century, 1920. *Project Gutenberg*. Web. 2 Nov. 2014.

Chapter 7. Lighting the Way

1. David E. Nye. *Electrifying America: Social Meanings of a New Technology*. Cambridge, MA: MIT Press, 1990. Print. 261.

2. Ibid.

3. Ibid. 307.

4. Ibid. 321.

5. "60-Watt Light Bulb Replacements." *GE Lighting*. General Electric Company, 2014. Web. 8 Mar. 2015.

6. Tracy Upton. "This Little Light of Mine: Understand Light Bulbs," *Earth Day*. Earth Day Network, n.d. Web. 8 Mar. 2015.

7. Whitney Matheson. "Photos: The Easy-Bake Oven Turns 50." *USA Today*. Gannett, 2 Oct. 2013. Web. 8 Mar. 2015.

Chapter 8. Electric Light Today

1. Cynthia Graber. "What a Difference a Light Bulb Makes." *Slate*. Slate Group, 22 Nov. 2013. Web. 3 Nov. 2014.

2. Rebecca Matulka and Daniel Wood. "The History of the Light Bulb." *Energy.gov*. US Department of Energy, 22 Nov. 2013. Web. 2 Jan. 2014.

3. Ibid.

4. "EPA Letter." *DarkSky.org*. International Dark-Sky Association, 30 July 2008. Web. 8 Mar. 2015.

5. David K. Randall. *Dreamland: Adventures in the Strange Science of Sleep*. New York: Norton, 2012. Print. 41.

6. Herbert Hoover. "246–Address on the 50th Anniversary of Thomas Edison's Invention of the Incandescent Electric Lamp." *American Presidency Project*. Gerhard Peters and John T. Woolley, 2015. Web. 8 March 2015.

7. Mark Lamster. "Say Goodbye to the Edison Bulb." *Details*. Condé Nast, 1 May 2011. Web. 8 Mar. 2015.

8. Rebecca Matulka. "Top Eight Things You Didn't Know about LEDs." *Energy.gov*. US Department of Energy, 4 June 2013. Web. 8 Mar. 2015.

9. Rebecca Matulka and Daniel Wood. "The History of the Light Bulb." *Energy.gov*. US Department of Energy, 22 Nov. 2013. Web. 8 Mar. 2015.

About the Author

Diane Bailey has written approximately 40 nonfiction books for teens on topics including sports, celebrities, government, finance, and technology. Her personal favorites are anything to do with history and culture, whether it be the development of dance, the society of ancient Greece, or the history of vampires. Bailey also works as a freelance editor. She has two sons and two dogs, and she lives in Kansas.